HOLD YOUR HORSES

HOLD YOUR HORSES

A FEEDBAG FULL

OF FACT AND FABLE

Milton Meltzer

HarperCollins*Publishers*

ACKNOWLEDGMENTS

Every effort has been made to locate the copyright holders of all copyrighted materials and secure permisson to reproduce them. In the event any question arises as to their use, the publisher will be glad to make changes in future printings and editions.

We gratefully acknowledge permission to publish the extract on page 73 from David Dary's *Cowboy Culture* (Knopf, 1981).

In addition we acknowledge the following individuals and institutions for the illustrations provided to us, and list the pages on which the illustrations appear.

Pages 29, 35, 52, 83: The Bettmann Archive; Page 22: The British Museum; Pages 64, 73: Amon Carter Museum, Fort Worth, Texas; Page 108: The Frick Collection; Pages 12, 18, 26, 28, 31, 33, 37, 54, 56, 60, 91, 92, 101, 103, 105: The Granger Collection; Pages 8–9: Laszlo Kubinyi; Page 88: The Metropolitan Museum of Art; Page 111: The Metropolitan Museum of Art, Gift of Irwin Untermyer, 1964; Pages 46, 89, 97, 107: New York Public Library Picture Collection; Page 98: Reuters/Bettman; Page 63: Smithsonian Institute National Anthropological Archives; Page 85: Salvatore Vitale, New York City Police Department.

Hold Your Horses!
A Feedbag Full of Fact and Fable
Copyright © 1995 by Milton Meltzer

Library of Congress Cataloging-in-Publication Data
Meltzer, Milton, date
  Hold your horses! : a feedbag full of fact and fable / Milton Meltzer
    p.   cm.
  Includes bibliographical references and index.
  ISBN 0-06-024477-1. — ISBN 0-06-024478-X (lib. bdg.)
  1. Horses—Juvenile literature.   2. Horses—History—Juvenile literature.
[1. Horses.]   I. Title.
SF302.M35   1995   95-2983
636.1—dc20   CIP
                                                                        AC

1   2   3   4   5   6   7   8   9   10
❖
First Edition

For Johnny and Jane

Contents

Introduction

When I was growing up, a long time ago, I can remember waking to the sound of a horse's hooves clattering over the cobblestones of our street. It was the milkman's horse, pulling a wagon loaded with wooden cases. The glass bottles clicked noisily against the metal strips that separated them. The milk was always delivered to our homes in the early morning hours, before most people were up for breakfast.

A horse pulled the iceman's wagon too. There was no electric refrigeration in those days. As the wagons came rumbling down the street, we kids ran out of our houses to ask for as big a chunk of ice as our mothers told us to get. We had to watch our step, so we wouldn't slip on the horse manure—mustard-brown clumps that steamed when they plopped down.

It's a great leap backward in time from the milkman's feeble nag to the horse of Darius the Great. Darius's horse was clever enough to make his master an emperor. As the story goes, there were several candidates for the throne of ancient Persia. They agreed that he should be king whose horse neighed first. Darius's horse obliged. It has been said that a single word has sometimes lost or won an empire. But Darius's horse proclaimed his master emperor without even speaking.

Another king, that wicked English tyrant depicted by Shakespeare in his play *Richard III*, was ready to give up his throne for a horse. "A horse! a horse! my kingdom for a horse!" he cries out at the Battle of Bosworth Field when his horse is slain and he stands alone against his enemies. He is offered a horse if he will flee, but he refuses to run, and is killed.

Where does that word *horse* come from? It derives from *hors* or *hross*, a word common to the old Germanic languages. *Webster's Tenth Collegiate Dictionary* defines it as "a large solid-hoofed herbivorous mammal domesticated since a prehistoric period and used as a beast of burden, a draft animal, or for riding."

There's lots more to the story of the horse than that. The horse has played a great role in human history from the most ancient of times down to today. Practically all young people— and many older ones, too—feel a deep affection for the horse, a love and respect shown in countless hours of care and protection. And why? For love of the horse's many qualities: its physical beauty, its noble bearing, its great spirit, its thrilling swiftness, and its long service to humankind.

ONE

Ancestors

"God forbid that I should go to any heaven in which there are no horses." One of President Theodore Roosevelt's friends wrote that to him.

That's what some people think of the horse. What do horses think? Of themselves? Of us? Unfortunately, we don't know, for horses do not keep diaries or write letters or give TV interviews. But men and women have observed horses closely for a very long time. A Greek soldier and historian named Xenophon wrote a book about the horse over two thousand years ago. After watching the animal's behavior, he and the many writers who followed him put together ideas about how horses think.

A herd instinct: that's the horse's strongest basic urge. Understandable when you realize that before horses were domesticated, their survival depended on sticking together. A group of horses had a better chance against predatory animals than one horse alone. The horses of today still like to be in company; it means security as well as companionship.

Like all herd animals, horses are followers. They look to a leader. They like a regular pattern of life. Familiar routine puts them at ease and makes them feel calm. The horse has a tightly tuned nervous system. It responds quickly to danger, but it also is excitable and nervous.

Horses are highly trainable. Their ability to race, jump, perform in horse shows, and carry out any number of tasks can be developed. Like people, horses must be willing to learn. (Again like us, if they're badly handled, they stubbornly refuse to learn.) For thousands of years they learned so much that their impact upon human history has been immense. From the dawn of prehistoric agriculture the horse has tilled the fields. Down through the ages, the horse has become an essential partner in warfare, in the exploration of strange territories, and in the hauling of raw materials to the factory and the finished product to the marketplace. Almost anything humans have demanded of it, the horse has done.

And done it because the horse is superbly equipped for so many tasks. Its strength, its speed, its vision, its hearing, its sense of smell, its reflexes—they are better than a human's. Its memory—a big factor in intelligence—is very good. It can learn the complex routine required of it in everything from circus acts to herding cattle on the range.

The personality of the horse varies considerably in individual horses and from one breed to another. There are hundreds of breeds and variations in color. Each horse has a basic character or temperament, with as many variations as are found among humans. Horses can be delightful or dull, energetic or listless, "good" or "bad." Some authorities believe that the horse is not by nature a brave animal. But those trained for warfare can display great courage in the face of terrible danger.

A horse's height is always described as so many "hands." Where did the form of measurement come from? Long before we had a system of feet and inches, horsemen measured the height of their animals in "hands." By that is meant the width of an adult male's hand, taken from the base of the thumb across the palm. That's been standardized as four inches. The horse is measured from the ground to the top of the shoulders. The "hand" measurement is used everywhere.

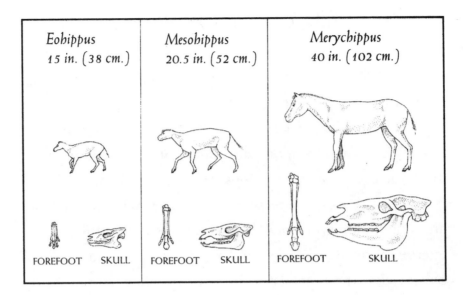

Eohippus 15 in. (38 cm.)	Mesohippus 20.5 in. (52 cm.)	Merychippus 40 in. (102 cm.)
FOREFOOT SKULL	FOREFOOT SKULL	FOREFOOT SKULL

Where did the horse family come from? When did this species of animal arrive? Its appearance on earth predates humankind.

The horse we know today—called *Equus caballus*—is the result of a long process of evolution that scientists have been able to trace through a series of fossilized skeletons dug up in North America and northern Europe at the beginning of the twentieth century. The earliest ancestor of the horse predates humans by about sixty million years. It's commonly called *eohippus*, the "dawn horse." It was a small animal, scarcely more than a foot high.

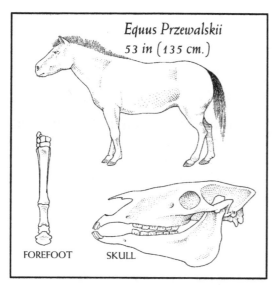

Equus Przewalskii
53 in (135 cm.)

FOREFOOT   SKULL

Reading this chart from left to right, you see how horses developed from epoch to epoch as they moved from region to region.

Although eohippus fossils are found in both the Old World and the New World, the evolution of the first horses took place chiefly in North America. Some of the forms that developed spread from North America into Asia and Europe, crossing by way of the land bridge (later flooded by the Bering Sea) that long ago connected Alaska with Siberia.

It was toward the end of the Pliocene Epoch, around 2,500,000 years ago, that the modern horse—*Equus*—evolved. As a new form it proved very successful. It spread from the plains of North America to South America and across the land bridge from Alaska to Siberia and all parts of Eurasia.

But a strange thing happened. The horse did very well in its North American homeland for millions of years. Then, about 10,000 years ago, it disappeared from North and South America. Why? No one is sure. Did devastating diseases or a fatal parasite wipe it out? Did humans who hunted horses kill them off? Were climatic changes to blame? The exhaustion of food supplies? The appearance of a natural enemy? When the Bering land bridge disappeared beneath the rising sea, it became impossible for the descendants of the horses that had migrated earlier to Asia to return to America. Not until the ships of the Spanish explorers carried them to the New World five hundred years ago did horses return to their native land.

It was during the evolution of *Equus* in Eurasia that local types of horses developed; all breeds descended from this single species, *Equus*. Eurasia's wide variations in climate, altitude, and soil influenced the evolution of the horse during these last ten thousand years. It explains the differences in size and shape we see in today's domestic horse.

Three of these prehistoric breeds are considered to be the ancestors of our domestic horses. One, called Przewalski's horse, evolved on the wild steppes of Turkestan in central Asia. It was about the size of a modern pony, with a thick neck and a short black mane that stuck straight up. A second breed, the forest horse, found in northern Europe, was the largest and heaviest. The steppe horse, the smallest of the three breeds, is thought to be the forerunner of what is now called the Arabian horse.

However, it would be a long time before people domesticated the horse. Their first use of the animal—over 100,000 years ago—was undoubtedly for food. They hunted the horse not only for meat but for hides.

How do we know what the ancient horse looked like? A hunting people called the Cro-Magnon lived in western Europe about 25,000 years ago. We owe our first glimpse of the horse to these people of the Upper Paleolithic period. Their paintings on the walls of caves in southern France, northern Spain, and North Africa or on slabs of stone in Scandinavia, as well as their engravings on bone and horn and their decoration of ceremonial objects, reveal the horses and other animals of their time. All three types of the early horse are depicted. The drawings suggest that horses were hunted and used only for food and clothing. The drawings of some animals may have been made to invoke success in the hunt for food.

Further evidence comes from the findings of geologists

exploring a Cro-Magnon camp at Solutré in France. In a wide circle surrounding the settlement, they dug up the bones of at least 100,000 horses, hunted down and used for food. Herds of these horses, about the size of today's pony, must have been tracked on their seasonal migration. The hunters massacred them in large numbers by chasing them over nearby cliffs.

It was around 3500 B.C. that some people discovered that not only could the horse be eaten, it could be used alive.

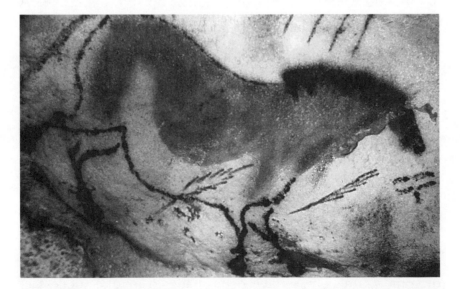

On the walls of the Lascaux cave in France, primitive men who hunted horses drew the animals between ten and twenty thousand years ago. Their artistry has survived, providing an invaluable record of some aspects of their lives.

Chariots and Conquerors

The horse was the last important animal to be domesticated. Cattle, sheep, goats, dogs, and pigs preceded it by thousands of years. Taming the horse, a giant step forward, seems to have been done first at a small settlement called Dereivka, in what is now Ukraine, on the southwestern end of the vast Asian-European steppes. There archaeozoologists unearthed evidence that these pastoral people kept herds of horses about 5,500 years ago. Why not round up the wild animals and keep them handy for meat when you needed it, or for hides, or for milk from the mares? They soon saw that the horse was stronger than the ass, faster than the ox, and more trainable than any other animals they knew. And who could resist climbing on the animal's back and galloping off?

These pastoral people were probably the first to tame and ride horses. They had also learned—from managing sheep, goats, and cattle—how to improve animals by care and selective breeding. The natural next step was to apply it to the horse. The result was a bigger and stronger animal, a horse that could not only supply meat and milk and hides, but pull loads as well.

But how best to use the horse's power? Only very gradually did ancient people discover that the best method of harnessing a horse for pulling a load was with either a breast band or a padded collar going around the whole neck—a form of the ox yoke.

At first the loads that horses pulled were placed in wagons with four solid wooden disc wheels. But solid wheels made the carts very heavy. The pastoral people found there was a limit to the weight of a vehicle a harnessed horse could pull. Many centuries later they learned to make lighter spoked wheels. It was a breakthrough invention leading to the fast, maneuverable chariot. Evidence for the evolution of the chariot was found in the early 1900s, when Russian archaeologists began systematic excavations at several sites east of the Ural Mountains. In burial grounds of elite people they found the remains of several chariots, probably the earliest ones developed anywhere.

That revolutionary change was made by the steppe culture around 2000 B.C. Before then, an oxcart could travel only two miles per hour, but now a chariot drawn by two

---

The horse was the center of great ceremony for the Scythians, who lived in a region around the Black Sea. When a king died, fifty of his young servants were strangled, and their bodies were gutted, stuffed with chaff, and sewn up again. Then fifty of the king's finest horses were given the same treatment. By elaborate means the bodies of the servants were affixed to the backs of the horses, and all were buried in honor of the king—in case he encountered his enemy in the next world.

The Chinese too, in prehistoric times, lived in a horse-based culture. Before 2000 B.C. their chieftains were buried with their horses, as excavation of tombs has revealed. In some places horse-and-chariot cemeteries have been unearthed. Hundreds of horses were buried in special graves. This suggests the Chinese thought of their horses as comrades, not servants.

horses could tear along at ten miles per hour. Imagine the delight of the charioteer as he whipped along the road!

Yet pleasure was only a minor effect of the chariot. Out of its invention came the development of chariot warriors. This made an enormous difference in world history. With the war chariot, military leaders were able to impose their power on centers of civilization throughout Asia and Europe. The chariot was probably used as a mobile shooting platform for archers. With charioteers at the reins, a mass of chariots would race forward while archers standing behind the drivers would shoot arrows at the enemy.

Military strategy began to be centered on chariotry, setting off an arms race. Rulers drained their treasuries to build more and more of the expensive chariots. They also had to maintain the costly chariot force. This required bows and arrows and a great host of specialists: horse trainers and grooms, saddlers, wheelwrights, harness makers, carpenters, veterinarians, and charioteers to drive, and warriors skilled in archery—plus clerks and quartermasters to keep track of it all.

With the right equipment and well-trained animals, nomadic people were ready to move anywhere at any time, fitted for aggressive warfare. John Keegan, a historian, believes that these nomadic warriors "must have been among the toughest people in creation."

The dwellers in settled lands could not resist attack by such mobile armies. Driving down from the highlands to the level plains, the invaders overran the foot soldiers of Mesopotamia and Egypt. In ten minutes ten chariots could cause over five hundred casualties—an enormous number for that time. The mobile warriors would take prisoners and make them slaves, using them as a source of unpaid labor.

The chariot dominated war-making not only in the Middle East but in other parts of the world too. A chariot industry and market emerged, for chariots were easy to duplicate, transport, and sell. The extent of their use depended mainly on the supply of good horses—not just any horses, but carefully selected and highly trained animals. Soon there were even manuals telling how to make chariots and train horses to pull them.

People learned fast or taught themselves. There is widespread evidence of military use of the horse and war chariot by the Kassites, Hurrians, and Hyksos in the Middle East, the Myceneans in Greece, and the Shang and Chou in China.

Engraved on a small scarab of the sixteenth century B.C. is a two-wheeled chariot carrying a pharaoh. Horses had been unknown to the Egyptians until the charioteers of the Hyksos, a Semitic people, conquered Egypt about 1700 B.C.

When the tomb of the young king Tutankhamen (c. 1350 B.C.) was excavated in Egypt in 1922, six chariots were found

Gold model of a chariot used by the Persians about 500 B.C.

among the great wealth of objects stored there. (They are now on display in a museum in Cairo.) The Egyptians probably were largely responsible for the spread of domesticated horses to other countries nearby. The Bible relates that when Joseph took his father's remains from Egypt back to Canaan, "there went up with him both chariots and horsemen" (Genesis 50:9).

Pictures of chariots cut into three stone stelae at Mycenae, dating around 1600 B.C., are the earliest sign of the horse's use in ancient Greece. There is literary evidence too, from the Greek poet Homer. His epic poem the *Iliad* tells how horses were used in the siege of Troy.

The most famous—and feared—charioteering people of ancient times were the Assyrians. Their kingdom was established about 1365 B.C. in Mesopotamia. Superb royal art, excavated at Nineveh and Nimrud, depicts the chariot at the heart of the armies that built an empire. Along a great network of royal roads, Assyrian mounted forces could move against enemies as fast as thirty miles a day.

The Assyrian rulers waged war year after year. They plundered other states, forced ransom and tribute, burned villages and towns, destroyed fields and orchards, massacred anyone who resisted, and enslaved others. Ashurnasirpal II, a terrible tyrant, in just one expedition in a small mountain district took 460 horses, 2,000 cattle, 5,000 sheep, and 15,000 prisoners, not to mention great wealth in copper, iron, silver, gold, grain, woolens, and linen. At the height of its domination, in the eighth century B.C., the Assyrian empire included parts of what are now Saudi Arabia, Iran, and Turkey, as well as all of modern Syria and Israel. The blameless horse had become the tool of men who invaded, destroyed, and enslaved.

THREE

From Nomads to Knights

Oddly, it was horses themselves that put the chariot warriors out of business. Although they were a key part of the chariot system, horses gradually became more important than the vehicles they pulled. Horses had been ridden for a long time before this—as early as 1350 B.C. But those mounted soldiers, depicted in Egyptian art, all rode bareback, without stirrups, and they straddled the horse well back on its rump—not a good position from which to control the animal. This suggests that the horses' backs may not yet have been strong enough to be ridden the modern way. But by the eighth century B.C. selective breeding had produced a horse that could be ridden from the forward seat,

A seal depicting Darius the Great, a Persian emperor, hunting lions from his chariot. The Persian charioteers were defeated by the cavalry of Alexander the Great in 331 B.C.

with the rider's weight over the shoulders. And horse and rider learned to work together so that men could use bows and arrows while in motion. Now mounted archers could use their skill against enemy troops.

Cavalry (from the Latin word *caballus*, horse) proved to be much more flexible than charioteers; they were able to maneuver in combat far more swiftly. It was such a mounted force that wrecked the power of the Assyrian charioteers. This force was a horse people known as the Scythians, riding out of east-central Asia beginning in the eighth century B.C. Horse-riding nomads like them would raid the outer edges of civilization in the Middle East, India, China, and Europe for hundreds of years.

The homeland of the nomads was a belt of steppes, or grassland, about 3,000 miles east to west and 500 miles north to south. To the north was subarctic territory; to the south, desert and mountains. This vast plain stretched from the river valleys of China in the east to the fertile lands of the Middle East and Europe in the west. The treeless plains of the steppe were great breeding grounds for cattle, sheep, goats—and horses.

The nomads liked their way of life, despising the labors of settled farmers. They enjoyed the freedom of horsemen; they hunted for food and shifted their tented dwellings with the seasons.

Why did the horse nomads invade other people's territory? One widely accepted theory is that the steppe could suffer sudden and disastrous climatic change. Warm, wet seasons made for good grazing, better for both animals and people. But such happy times were often followed by drought and hard times, when people and their herds of animals went hungry. Migrating within the steppe wouldn't help because neighbors suffered in the same way, and besides, they resisted invasion. So the obvious way to escape trouble was to move farther out, riding into a gentler climate where cultivated land could provide food for all.

Another motive for nomadic invasion was that it was a way to force more highly developed peoples to trade. The steppe people had horses and slaves to exchange for the manufactured goods that merchants could supply.

Of all the conquerors who fought on horseback, rather than from chariots, the most famous was Alexander the Great (356–323 B.C.). He learned to ride at an early age and, from the time he was ten, was taught the intelligence of horses in the art of war by his father, King Philip of Macedonia. When he was only sixteen, Alexander was given command over Philip's cavalry at the Battle of Chaeronae. At twenty, upon the death of his father, Alexander succeeded to the throne and put down uprisings in the cities of Greece over which his father had ruled. He then undertook the war against Persia that Philip had been planning. Alexander's military achievements during the brief years of his career were spectacular, and they were carried out mostly on horseback. (Chariots had long been out of fashion in Greece.) Alexander's army relied on regiments of armored horsemen who wielded spears and swords. His cavalry and infantry numbered some 50,000—an enormous army in that day. He met the Persians under King Darius in three great battles, and he destroyed that imperial army's war chariots. In search of new lands to conquer, he advanced as far as the plains of northern India.

Often Alexander's horsemen met enemies who also rode

One of the most famous horses in history was Bucephalus. He was brought to King Philip of Macedonia, who was looking for a new battle charger. When Philip's royal trainer rejected the horse as too vicious, Philip's young son, Alexander, pleaded to be allowed to have the beautiful horse. Yes, said the king, but only if you can ride him here and now. To the astonishment of Philip and the court, the boy mounted the horse and rode off. When Bucephalus had been paraded before the king, Alexander alone had noticed that a shadow had frightened the horse. Turning Bucephalus away from the shadow, he was able to control him. Bucephalus carried Alexander the Great to many victories, until the horse was killed in action. Alexander named a town after him.

In this detail from a Roman mosaic at Pompeii, Alexander the Great, a cavalry genius, is depicted fighting on horseback.

horses. But even when his soldiers were outnumbered by the enemy's cavalry, Alexander gained victory by the resourceful way he used his cavalry. Mounted soldiers would strike the first blow against the enemy line in a frontal assault that threw the opposition into confusion. His cavalry would also try to outflank the enemy, cutting off possible lines of retreat, and separating the enemy forces from the sources of supply.

Alexander might have been the first to build a world empire, but fever brought him down, and he died at the age of thirty-three. His brilliant tactics using horses earned the admiration of great military leaders down through the centuries.

Seven centuries after the time of Alexander the Great, riding horses carried a great wave of Central Asian conquerors into the Western world. They were called the Huns—a name that came to strike terror in the popular mind. They were steppe horsemen who invaded the Roman Empire in the fifth century A.D.

The horse the Huns rode was a shaggy steppe pony. It had short legs, a thick neck, a pot belly, a convex face, and a stiff mane. Small and dun-colored, it was common throughout southern Russia and Central Asia.

The Huns spoke a Turkic language, had no writing, and practiced a form of nature worship called animism. Why did they wage war so much? As nomads they were a hardy people, used to moving about easily. They lived by raiding rather than planting. They had no religious taboos against killing or enslaving others. They found that war was profitable (for the winners, of course).

After each conquest the Huns took slaves and sold them off, never hesitating to break up families to maximize profit. Another huge source of their wealth came from ransoming military and civilian captives for gold.

The most notorious Hun was one of their kings, Attila, called the Scourge of God. For many years he extorted great

In this oil painting, Attila, the Scourge of God, leads his cavalry into combat.

tribute from the Romans. In 451 he invaded Gaul—now France—with half a million Huns and allies. Defeated in battle, he turned back and invaded Italy. Before he could reach Rome, a shortage of supplies and the outbreak of a devastating epidemic in his army caused him to quit. He died soon afterward of a nosebleed.

Cavalry dominated warfare for hundreds of years. Soldiers on horseback proved their superiority in breaking up the Roman Empire. The Romans had bred horses mostly for sport and recreation, not for military use. In battle they relied on foot soldiers, with cavalry only a supporting force.

It cost them defeat after defeat, as the cavalries of invaders—Persians, Goths, and Visigoths—proved to be decisive.

It would be hard to overstate the role of the horse in the history of Islam, the religion of which Mohammed was the prophet. (It is now the principal religion in many parts of the world. Believers are called Moslems or Muslims.) In its first hundred years—from the early seventh century on—Islam spread with an amazing speed, made possible by a new breed of horse, the Arabian.

Mohammed, the founder of Islam, in this miniature is depicted on horseback, watched over by the Angel Gabriel.

Mohammed himself kept a large herd of trained horses. His Arabian steeds are said to have been bred by the nomadic Bedouins of the Middle East's desert region. His own favorite was a stallion named Al Borak. The Bedouin herdsmen developed horses of great beauty, speed, and endurance. Arabian horses are medium to small in size, with a long and graceful neck, and are predominantly bay, gray, or chestnut, or occasionally white or black. Arabians were developed primarily as saddle horses. Their riders carried Islam across North Africa, across the Straits of Gibraltar, and up into Spain and France as far as Poitiers. There, in A.D. 732, they were stopped by the Frankish cavalry. In Spain Muslims continued to prosper for many centuries, exerting a great influence on that country's history and culture. They were finally driven out when the rulers Ferdinand and Isabella united Spain and defeated them at Granada.

But they had left a lasting imprint. The Arabian horse and the Muslim saddle, stirrup, style of riding, and use of cavalry in combat were adopted in much of Christian Europe. And the traits of this superb animal would be absorbed by the many other breeds it sired.

A new direction in horse breeding led to another change in warfare. The Goths and the Vandals in northern Germany started to breed horses heavier than the small, light ones that the Huns and other armies of the steppes were using. By the eighth century cavalry fighting on lightweight horses was ending in Europe. Cavalry fighters were succeeded by armored knights. Often the knight and his armor weighed 350 to 425 pounds. The knights rode horses of great size, strength, and endurance. These heavyweight chargers were also protected by armor—heavy steel skirting and headgear devised to protect the animal. This is why the light Arabian

An armored knight of Prato, Italy, astride his great war horse. From an illuminated manuscript of the fourteenth century.

horse wouldn't do; only the heavy breed of horse could carry the weight.

These great warhorses were trained to maneuver in mock combat or in battle to the death. They were ridden by aristocrats called the *chivalry* (a name taken from *cheval*, the French word for horse), who made up the small armies of the medieval era. Accompanying them in battle were squires, pages, servants, and yeomen, all as foot soldiers. In medieval sieges the ponderous and powerful warhorses were used as tanks are used today. A pair of horses wearing blinders was driven at a clanking gallop against a studded castle door. The force of their weight could sometimes smash it off its hinges.

Is a poet worth as much as a horse? Not always, not even when he is one of the world's great poets. Chaucer, fighting in the English army, was captured by the French and held for ransom. King Edward III paid £16 to get his poet safely returned, but paid £20 ransom to get back a warhorse. One historian sourly noted that there has never been a period in history when the average man could bring the price of a good horse.

A medieval tournament, with knights fighting knights on horseback.

War was so much the way of life for medieval aristocrats that it even shaped their recreation. The joust, their favorite sport, was a single contest between two knights, packed into armor and hoisted aboard their big mounts. At a given signal, they raced at each other, each trying to unseat his adversary by poking him with a long lance. It was a disaster to be unhorsed. The jousts were features of elaborate tournaments held at the invitation of kings and nobles. In the pavilions alongside the tournament field sat the judges and the ladies who sponsored their champions. Heralds announced the names of the contestants, and then, with a fanfare of trumpets, the warriors made their entrance, riding elaborately caparisoned horses. A Queen of Beauty awarded the prizes to the winners. Often knights and their horses were injured or killed in the tournaments. No matter: It was all part of this game, a game that was popular from the eleventh to the sixteenth century. Sir Walter Scott's novel *Ivanhoe* is a captivating story of the days of chivalry.

Both horses and men have long been subject to the military draft. In the fourteenth century, for one of England's many invasions of France, 8,000 carts were built to order, each of them to be drawn by four horses. Villages all over England were obliged to produce the 32,000 horses needed.

The crash of gunfire ended the age of chivalry. But the introduction of gunpowder did not end the use of cavalry. As long-range, rapid-fire guns were perfected, cavalry charges often became disasters. Tennyson's poem "The Charge of the Light Brigade" captures the horror of the suicidal British cavalry charge under the guns of the Russian artillery at Balaklava in the Crimean War of the 1850s:

Cannon to the right of them,
Cannon to the left of them,
Cannon in front of them
Volleyed and thundered . . .
Into the mouth of Hell
Rode the six hundred.

Only five years after that war ended, the horse would face unbelievable suffering in another war, on the far side of the Atlantic.

The famed "Charge of the Light Brigade" in the Crimean War of 1854, from an engraving. The British cavalry were driven out of the Valley of Death by Russian forces.

FOUR

A Terrible Price to Pay

Although cavalry would play a lesser role in warfare in the 1800s, its use continued. From the first battle to the last, the American Civil War (1861–1865) was powered by the horse. Both sides depended on field artillery and cavalry, every infantry unit required supply wagons, and wounded soldiers prayed for ambulance wagons to get them to the medics. Which is why horses were a primary target of that conflict.

If you look at the innumerable photographs or sketches of Civil War battlefield scenes, you'll see horse carcasses scattered all over the ground. Union commanders reported that Confederate sharpshooters killed or wounded an average of five hundred horses a day. Take just one cavalry unit—the

First Vermont. Their state raised more purebred horses than any other state in the North. Those horses, called Morgans, provided the First Vermont cavalry unit with the only mounts equal to the Thoroughbreds of the South. One thousand

Stonewall Jackson, the Confederate cavalry commander, was shot and killed accidentally by one of his own men during the Battle of Chancellorsville in Virginia on May 2, 1863.

Morgans were ridden into combat; only two hundred survived.

The cavalry was not of prime importance in the fighting, however. It was needed for scouting and raiding, but its role in combat was not decisive. Union and Confederate cavalry units often met in skirmishes that sometimes turned into pitched battles. But only rarely did cavalry fight infantry. Yet to the press and the public the horse warriors seemed glorious. With their dash and daring, the cavalrymen had the aura of knights in shining armor.

Throughout the first half of the four-year war the Confederate cavalry did much better than the Union cavalry. For in this respect the South had the advantage in background and tradition. Most Johnny Rebs were country boys, used to horses, trained to the saddle from childhood. They understood horses and knew how to care for them. When a man joined the cavalry, he brought his own horse with him.

True, a large number of Billy Yanks in the cavalry were farm boys too. But most horses in the North were draft animals, not saddle horses. Despite their ignorance of horses, the glamor of the cavalry drew many city-bred men to the mounted troops. It took a long time for such volunteers to become first-class riders, especially with poor horses under them. They often rode nags that unscrupulous traders palmed off on the army.

Although Confederate cavalrymen had their own horses, if they lost their mounts, they could not get others from the army; they had to find their own replacements. That meant going back home on furlough. As the heavy losses of the war mounted, many men lost heart and simply disappeared.

When opposing cavalry occasionally met in the full shock of battle, there was lightning-fast action—the air ringing with the clash of saber on saber, the noise of guns going off, and the neighing and screaming of frightened horses. The Union cavalry gradually acquired the most modern firearms, small rifles ideal for use in close quarters. When their single-shot weapons gave way to repeating rifles, vast numbers of casualties resulted among the Confederates.

By 1864 Sheridan and Sherman, Union commanders, had well-seasoned cavalry at their command. On the move to Virginia, General Sheridan's army included 10,000 mounted men, making a column 13 miles long. In the west, General Sherman took 15,000 cavalrymen on his drive to Atlanta, and 5,000 on his march to the sea.

One of the most famous cavalry officers on either side was Nathan Bedford Forrest. "Forrest is the very devil," wrote

General Sherman. Sherman was determined to hound the Confederate leader "to the death, if it cost 10,000 lives and break the Treasury. There will never be peace in Tennessee till Forrest is dead."

Forrest was a rough, illiterate slave trader from Memphis, Tennessee. He enlisted in the Confederate army as a private in 1861, and in two years rose to the rank of major general. He introduced a new twist in cavalry tactics. His men moved swiftly in surprise attacks, and when they had cornered the enemy, they leaped off their horses to fight on foot. A ruthless man, Forrest demanded total surrender—no conditions. When the Union commander at Fort Pillow, a Mississippi River post held by African-American troops, refused to give up, Forrest stormed the garrison. After the surrender, he let his troops massacre the black soldiers.

Forrest survived the war to become Grand Dragon of the newly formed Ku Klux Klan, an underground army of white supremacists whose legacy of violent racism continues to haunt America.

The loss of horses and mules in the Civil War was twice as great as human mortality. The death toll of soldiers, sailors, and marines on both sides was 618,000. Between 1,2000,000 and 1,500,000 horses and mules are estimated to have died in service.

With even greater advances in technology, such as automatic weapons, the fate of the horse in wartime approached mass murder. In just one day's battle in World War I (1914–1918), 7,000 horses were killed. The British sent a million horses into that conflict; only 62,000 survived. Even

Military historians have recorded thousands of battles decided by a cavalry charge. You wonder—how did the horses stand the shock and noise and terror of battle? Horses are by nature herd animals, timid, shy, and not at all aggressive. Yet in combat they would respond to commands alien to their gentle temperament and native sweetness. The answer lies partly in selective breeding, and partly in training. With proper methods horses could be induced to brave the clash of combat. The training required lots of skill, time, and energy.

Experts point out that horses don't fear death—simply because, like all other nonhuman creatures, they have no idea of death. Warhorses were unaware that if they survived one battle, they would be made to endure still more.

though they knew how helpless horses were in modern warfare, the Polish army tried one final desperate cavalry charge in 1939, in the first days of Hitler's invasion of their homeland. The tanks and dive-bombers of the Nazis wiped them out. After more than two thousand years, it was the end of the warhorse. The obedient animal had paid a terrible price for its domestication by man.

FIVE

Human Muscle— or Horse Power

Until they domesticated animals, humans had only their own strength to rely on when it came to getting work done. Yet man with his muscle is a pretty poor engine. Measured in horsepower, a man's strength is a joke. To do the hauling one horse can do, it takes the strength of ten men. A farm boy driving a four-horse team hitched to a gangplow can do as much work as if each horse were replaced by forty men.

So when the horse—attached to the plow, wagon, or carriage—entered everyday life, it marked a great change. There was no romance in this life compared to war chariots, cavalry charges, or medieval tournaments. No, this was drudgery, especially for the horse: dull routine it had to adapt to. Horses always adapt to whatever task they are assigned to.

In Europe, even as late as the 1700s, use of horses was limited mainly to the upper class. Or to people who needed horses to do the chores of their employers. This was even true of transport by stagecoach, for the price was pretty high. The poor had to get around on foot.

In our time of motorized transport, it is hard to conceive of a world without cars, buses, and trucks. But try to put yourself back into eighteenth-century Europe. Every great

---

What price the horse? The answer is influenced by many considerations, among them demand, rarity, and intended use. Moroccan horses were once a great luxury, bartered for gold dust, ivory, and slaves in the Sudan. Around A.D. 1500 a horse sold for twelve slaves; later, for only five. In the nineteenth century in North Africa a good horse could fetch fifty ducats, while a slave eighteen years old went for sixteen ducats and a child sold for seven. During the Renaissance good horses brought high prices in Europe. The guard of 2,000 horses maintained by Cosimo de Medici in Florence was so expensive, it ruined him. In the eighteenth century in Europe the price of horses fell because there was an oversupply.

city—London, Paris, St. Petersburg, Madrid, Vienna—was full of stables. The blacksmith was an important man, running a business like a modern car-repair garage. City dwellers depended on horses for their daily provisions and for getting about from place to place. There were proportionately as many horses in Paris as there are automobiles today. If you were in a hurry, and could afford it, you hired a carriage. There were two thousand of them roving the congested streets of Paris, and they were as hard to catch in rush hour as taxis are now. The cabs were dilapidated, the horses broken-down nags, and the coachmen foulmouthed. City horses had to be fed; there was a big business in supplying oats, barley, hay, and straw, with provisioners as common as gas stations today.

In the time that Jane Austen was writing her great English novels, horses were commonplace. During most of the year the roads and paths were too dirty for her to walk. If she wished to go even a few miles, she had to ride a horse or ride in a vehicle pulled by a horse. She couldn't go to a ball except in a carriage. People in society were judged by their mode of travel. Just as today we know the difference in class between a Chevy and a Cadillac, so Jane Austen could tell the rank of her visitors by a glance at the horse and carriage.

A procession of the Four-in-Hand Club drives through New York's Central Park on the way to the racetrack in Jerome Park in 1875.

In colonial America, too, the early settlers of New England believed that horses belonged to the gentry. Cattle, sheep, and pigs were more useful to the farmers and villagers. The only horse reported in Plymouth Colony in 1632 was a mare ridden by Governor William Bradford. By 1649 there were some two hundred horses in New England. A horse cost three times as much as an ox or cow. Faster than oxen, horses were used as pack animals on the narrow forest trails, especially in snowy winter weather. Pack trains of horses carried supplies and household goods from one community to the founding of another as settlers moved on. In clear weather, when the ice was thick enough on the waterways, horses could haul passengers on frozen rivers, going as far as fifty miles in ten hours. In the mid-1600s both horses and skilled riders began to migrate to America from Ireland. The men chanted an ancient Irish minstrel song: "Three glories of a gathering are: a beautiful wife, a good horse, and a swift hound."

For quite some time, however, sturdy oxen continued to draw the plow in New England. Horses were used mostly as pack animals, for riding, and later to pull wagons and stagecoaches. Not until about 1840 were horses hitched to buggies.

In the colonial South, as tobacco and cotton crops spread, planters bought saddle horses so they could ride over their large estates. By 1770 the rich began to import racing horses from England. George Washington maintained a large horse-breeding farm at Mount Vernon.

Another president, Andrew Jackson, not only bred horses but owned a racetrack. He would bet as much as $5,000—a huge sum in those days—on one of his own horses. His racing stable earned him more than $20,000 in prize money.

The Dutch, Puritans, and Quakers in the North disapproved of horse racing. They stuck to farming, importing heavier breeds of horses to do hard work. They hitched them to giant wagons to carry freight overland. Both horses and wagons were called Conestogas, after the valley of that name in Pennsylvania. The Conestoga wagon was the first freight car of its time, drawn by four-, six-, or eight-horse teams.

By 1750 there were seven thousand Conestoga wagons in use in Pennsylvania. They were a dazzling sight—the wagon bodies painted a bright blue, the wheels scarlet, and the linen hood, arched over the body, white. Throughout the American Revolution the red-white-and-blue Conestoga horse teams hauled commissary and artillery supplies. Later, they carried pioneers west on the new turnpikes.

Stopping at taverns on the road, the wagonmen sang verses they made up to a folk tune:

> *It's a-rainin', it's a-hailin',*
> *The moon gives no light.*
> *Your horses can't travel*
> *This dark lonesome night.*

As the pioneers ventured beyond Pittsburgh, on into the Middle West, the covered wagons were slimmed down for faster passage of the families they carried across the prairies, and their colors were toned down to quieter browns and greens. These were the first prairie schooners. They were used to open up vast countries—not only the U.S., but Australia and South Africa—to migrating peoples.

By the 1830s teamsters dominated the roads linking the American cities. They piled their big wagons high with boxes, crates, barrels, and bales. It was slow going. A six-horse team hauling a four-ton load took all day to cover twenty-five miles. Whenever it rained or snowed, or when droves of cattle, sheep, or hogs got in the way, the roads jammed up. About fifteen thousand men worked as full-time teamsters, living most of their days and nights on the road, much like today's long-haul truck drivers.

Earlier, in colonial times, it was Benjamin Franklin who made use of the horse to pioneer a dependable system of mail deliveries. As the King's Postmaster General for the North, he recruited young horsemen to work as postriders. He guaranteed year-round deliveries between Philadelphia and Boston. It took a rider a week, covering over forty miles a day, to ride from one city to the other. Franklin was also the first to set up stone posts as highway mile markers, so travelers would know how far they'd gone. He induced several of the colonies to improve the construction and maintenance of highways, getting stumps and stones out of the way, laying logs across swampy sections, and building bridges over creeks. Horses then had an easier time pulling wagons, carriages, and stagecoaches.

The coach was a kind of boxy wagon used as an enclosed private carriage. (It was invented around 1400 in central Europe.) It seated four passengers; the driver sat outside, perched above the front wheels. Around 1740, Moravians in Bethlehem, Pennsylvania, started the first weekly coach service in America. It ran to and from Philadelphia. Soon one enterprising businessman launched another line, linking Philadelphia and New York. It took three days to travel the hundred miles. Later, four-horse teams speeded up service, making the run in forty-eight hours.

At first most horses were not shod. The horny casing on a horse's foot was enough to protect it. However, when the old dirt roads were surfaced with cobblestones, bricks, or planks, they injured the horses' hooves. The casing wore away and broke when the animals traveled on hard surfaces. A rim of iron, adjusted to the shape of the horse's hoof, took care of the problem. Blacksmiths soon learned how to trim hooves, hammer out the right size and shape of the shoes, and fit them securely. Their shops became the center of town life along the highways. One development led to another: As the sale of horse-drawn vehicles went up, so did wagon manufacturing, which in turn provided work for wheelwrights, turners, harness makers, and other parts suppliers.

Nevertheless, most Americans around 1800 still traveled primarily on foot. For one thing, they didn't need to go far. They stayed in their own communities, which were country neighborhoods of about thirty farms, where they passed their daily lives. When they wished to go into the village—to the store, tavern, or church—maybe once a week, or even just once a month, they walked. In New England, little children often walked two or more miles to school, and young people working away from home as farm laborers or schoolteachers might walk ten miles to spend Sunday with their family.

Certainly the great majority of urban dwellers owned no horses, but even in regions where horses were widely used for farm work, many people didn't own them. Instead, they offered their labor or farm produce to better-off folk in exchange for borrowing horses for plowing, hauling, or traveling.

A horsecar running on rails in a New York City street.

Often two or even three family members would ride on the back of one horse plodding along a country road on the way to church or the village store. But by 1830 that old gray mare hitched to a wagon had become the most common road vehicle. The wagon was used for farm work and to haul produce or goods, as well as to carry the family around. Ma and Pa would sit on kitchen chairs placed up front, while the kids squatted on straw in the back.

Even New York City had no public transportation until 1827, when Abraham Bowers put the first horsecar on the streets. It seated twelve people. Five years later the city was the first in the world to boast of a horsecar running on rails similar to later trolley car tracks. Built like a stagecoach, the horsecar seated ten people and ran on Fourth Avenue between Prince and Fourteenth streets. Horsecars soon spread across the country. By 1860 there were five hundred miles of horsecar lines in major cities.

In the cities milk, ice, coal, wood, and other necessities were delivered to the home by horse-drawn wagons, while butcher boys on nags brought the housewife her meat supply. Horses were also crucial to transport on the canals that laced the countryside in the early nineteenth century. They

In this 1837 painting by George Harvey, horses tow a barge along the Erie Canal in upstate New York.

plodded along the towpaths, pulling long barges loaded with freight. And peddlers bringing all kinds of small goods got about the country on horseback. By 1860 there were more than sixteen thousand of them going door to door, farmhouse to farmhouse.

Far more colorful than these essential but routine chores was a spectacular task assigned the horse in the West. In story, memoir, and movie the Pony Express has entered American mythology. It began in 1859, when the Kentuckian Alexander Majors organized the rapid delivery of mail on horseback. Majors recruited only "young, skinny, wiry fellows, not over 18, willing to risk death daily." These riders carried letters from St. Joseph, Missouri, to Sacramento, California—a distance of some 1,800 miles—in ten days. Remount stations were placed along the route at intervals of seven to twenty miles, and each rider covered about 75 miles before handing on his letter mailbag to the next man—or rather boy!

Nevada was the wildest and bloodiest link in the Pony Express route, and several riders had been picked off by Indians who resisted the invasion of their lands. In desperation, Majors hired Charlie Miller, only eleven years old but

A Pony Express rider tears off to the next postal station on his rugged route.

an experienced rider and a dead shot. On his very first ride in 1860, Indians came at him from the front and rear. Drawing his two guns, Charlie shot in both directions at once and managed to escape.

Majors, a humane man, had his employees sign a good-conduct oath that ran, in part:

> I agree not to use profane language, not to get drunk, not to gamble, not to treat animals cruelly, and not to do anything incompatible with the conduct of a gentleman. I agree, if I violate any of the above conditions, to accept my discharge without any pay for my services.

The mounts used by the Pony Express were mostly Western-reared horses, for these were bred to be able to run at full speed almost continuously. But there were so many obstacles to overcome along the way—washed-out trails, blizzards, cyclones, prairie fires, snow-covered passes, hostile Indians—that the mail rarely made its destination on schedule. Nonetheless, Bob Haslam will always be remembered as the Pony Express rider who in 1861 galloped across the plains carrying President Lincoln's first inaugural address to the Western outposts.

The Pony Express failed to make a profit, and when the telegraph line to the Pacific Coast was completed in October of 1861, its brief, romantic day ended. The Pony Express lasted only eighteen months, from the spring of 1859 to the fall of 1861.

A Revolution in Indian Life

Let's go back 500 years to the time when horses returned to the Americas. Remember that the horse had disappeared from the western hemisphere about 9,500 years before. The horses came back carried in the ships of Christopher Columbus on his second voyage. His aim on this trip was to build a permanent colony on Hispaniola, the island in the Caribbean that now includes both Haiti and the Dominican Republic. Horses, as well as pigs, sheep, and cattle, were among the first animals Columbus brought for breeding.

After a hundred days of sailing across three thousand miles of rough seas—probably the longest ocean shipment of a herd of large animals up to that point in history—the animals were pushed overboard to swim to shore on the coast of Haiti.

The horse latitudes is the name for those permanent belts of high atmospheric pressure that encircle the globe 30 degrees north and south of the equator. How did the horse nose into the weather report? One tradition says that when sailing vessels carrying horses to New World colonies were becalmed in the zones, the animals went ship-crazy and died.

In 1521, Ponce de León landed horses in Florida. French explorers sent horses ashore in Canada in 1541. In 1585, Sir Walter Raleigh sent horses from England to his colony of Roanoke in Virginia. Around 1600 the Spanish began to establish a chain of Catholic missions that ran from the eastern coast of Mexico up the Rio Grande, then across the mountains to the Pacific Coast. The priests brought along horses as they established each mission among the Indians.

In the early days of the conquest of the Americas, horses were perhaps even more important than firearms. Hernán Cortés had only sixteen horses (ten stallions, five mares, and a foal) when he invaded Mexico in 1519. The native inhabitants, who had never seen either white people or horses, were amazed at the strange spectacle. Some thought these men in armor astride horses were a new kind of

*The Spanish conquistadors who brought horses to the Americas, as depicted in
an Indian codex, c. 1534.*

beast—dragons or centaurs. Others were appalled to hear
that "deer" bearing strange beings on their backs, "as high as
rooftops," were coming to attack them. They were told that
the horses could catch anyone whom they ran after and that
the guns could kill from a distance anyone the invaders
wished, to which one Indian leader remarked, "Well, they
must be gods then."

The Spaniards took advantage of their shock and repre-
sented themselves as instruments of divine power, sent to

rule the earth. The Indians, however, soon found the horse, that strange beast, was an easy target for sword or lance or arrow, and that it died as readily as its rider.

Throughout their colonies in the Americas the Spaniards did not allow Indians to own horses. The penalty for stealing a horse was death by hanging. Nevertheless, the Indians who were enslaved to labor for the Spaniards in stables and on ranches quickly learned how to ride and train horses. Frequently slaves would run off with horses. Sometimes the Indians kidnapped colonial officials and ransomed them for horses. To get still more, Indians rode onto the range and ran off many horses at once. Some tribes learned to breed superior stock, and raced horses for fun.

After 1600, horses became the prized possessions of many of the tribes of the Great Plains—the Apache, the Blackfoot, the Cheyenne, the Ute, the Kiowa, and the Pawnee. The Comanche won a reputation for the best horsemanship, and the Cayute and the Nez Percé demonstrated the greatest skill in breeding horses. Many Indian tribes ate horses at first, but they stopped when they found the animals much more useful for hunting and transportation.

The Indian demand for horses shot way up. Horses were stolen not only from the Spanish but from other Indians and became a major cause of the perpetual raids the Plains tribes made on each other. Stealing a tethered horse from the camp of an enemy was like winning a badge of honor. One expert states that "probably a hundred times as many horses changed owners by theft as by trade."

Settlers moving west in the 1850s began to run across bands of wild horses created when tribal camps were attacked by hostile tribes and horses fled, escaping capture.

Pers Crowell, *a mid-twentieth-century artist known for his work on Indian themes, said this:*

The Indians were perhaps the first to use the art of camouflage; by choosing the colored horse that blended in best with the seasonal and geographic background, they could make themselves less conspicuous. White horses were used when snow lay on the ground; dun-coated horses were used in the fall to blend in with dried prairies; blue roans effectively blended into sagebrush backgrounds; pintos and grays were favored more than all others because their body colors could be easily altered by smearing or dyeing to suit the surroundings.

Navajo Indians ride through the Canyon de Chelly in Arizona. A 1904 photograph by Edward S. Curtis.

Among the Indians of the Plains region, where differences in wealth and rank had hardly existed before, the more horses a man had, the higher his standing. Horses were the most common property exchanged for a bride. Many tribes killed a horse or a dog when the owner died, as a sacrifice to the supernatural. When a Blackfoot chief died in 1834, 150 horses were slaughtered in his honor and buried near his grave.

A buffalo hunt on the Western plains, as imagined by the painter Charles Russell in 1899.

The Indians became famous expert horsemen. Because they used no saddles, they became "a part of the horse." They needed both hands for shooting arrows at animal or human targets while riding at a forty-mile-an-hour gallop, so they learned to guide their mounts by shifting their weight and by using knee pressure.

From boyhood, every Plains Indian man was trained to fight on horseback. In the wars fought with U.S. troops, the Indians earned a reputation as the world's best cavalrymen.

The coming of the horse revolutionized Indian life on the plains and prairies. It changed not only the way they fought but also the way they hunted buffalo—the main source of their food, clothing, fuel, and shelter. On horseback they became fast-moving nomads, and hunting the buffalo became easier and more profitable. Village life was given up in favor of wandering in pursuit of the migratory buffalo herds. This in turn increased contact with whites, as the buffalo hunters supplied fur traders with meat. There was a lively trade in buffalo tongues and tallow, too, and as beaver fur lost its importance, buffalo robes became a major article in the fur trade.

Of course Indians traded horses, too. But they found capturing horses far more fun than trading for them.

Horse-trading is an ancient business going back as far as prebiblical times. Different types of horses were raised in various parts of the world. The need for horses that could not to be found locally led to trading across frontiers. (It led to wars of conquest, too, when warriors took by force the horses they preferred.)

The greatest horse trader of them all was King Solomon. The ruler of the ancient Hebrews kept 1,200 saddle horses and 40,000 chariot horses in his royal stables. This he did despite the Hebrew injunction against keeping horses as a form of idolatry.

In the time of the Persian ruler Xerxes, dealers drove 25,000 horses a year on the 500-mile journey from Armenia into Persia. And later the number doubled and doubled again—a huge trade in horses. The Armenian breed was strong and fast, ideal for the Persian cavalry. Horses bred in Naples and Andalusia were so highly prized at one time that they could not be bought without special permission from the kings of those lands. (This led to smuggling, naturally.) Rich lords had their agents scouring the horse markets of Europe for good buys. Some noblemen made deals with pirates or thieves to get the horses they desired.

SEVEN

The Cowboy's Golden Age

Horse and cowboy—they are inseparable in American history and myth. The connection goes back 500 years, to the time when Columbus and the subsequent Spanish adventurers brought both horses and cattle to the New World. Their aim was to find gold, but when the promise of instant wealth was not fulfilled, many turned to breeding horses and cattle. In Mexico especially, Spaniards grazed cattle on the grass-covered plains and valleys. With cattle multiplying almost unbelievably fast on the common grazing grounds, rustling increased too. Who would guard the cattle? The Spaniards refused to do it—labor was beneath their dignity, as it was for the priests who raised cattle on their mission lands.

The padres solved the problem by training their new converts—mostly Indians and imported Africans—to ride horses and to care for the cattle. It was the beginning of a new occupation—the cowboy, or *vaquero*, as he was called in Spanish. The vaqueros were not admired as romantic figures. To the Spaniards they were only poor workers on horseback. They lived under miserable conditions; they wore ragged old clothing they found for themselves, and they slept on the ground or in rough lean-tos. While out on the range, they ate beef or wild game when they could, but more often, their meals were just cooked corn mush.

The early vaqueros usually rode stallions, for the male horse was stronger than the mare. They claimed they could judge a stallion's power by the size of its testicles and the loudness of its neigh. Because many stallions and mares strayed, wild horses became so common that a man could have a horse of his own if he bothered to capture and tame an animal.

But even more plentiful than the wild horses were wild cattle. They too strayed from the watchful eye of the vaquero. Wild cattle were so hard to control that ranchers regularly rounded them up just to get them used to people. This custom, begun in the 1550s, was called the *rodeo*, from a Spanish word for "encircle." It was a routine activity, with none of the razzle-dazzle of rodeos in the modern American West.

The primary working tool for the vaquero early on was the lasso (*lazo* in Spanish), a rope with a slipknot. Looped around the cow's horns, the rope was then pulled taut, and the animal was thrown to the ground, for branding or killing.

Just as there would be later in the American West, there were roving bands of lawless men who called themselves vaqueros but who robbed and terrorized people anywhere they liked. Because labor was so scarce, ranchers were often forced to hire these bandits on horseback to move large herds of cattle from one district to another.

About 100 years after the Spaniards invaded the Americas, wars in Europe caused Spain to suffer bad times. To raise desperately needed money, the king of Spain gave wealthy ranchers huge tracts of land—for a price. Often it was land the rancher had already occupied, but without royal approval. Now, with the king's legal authority backing him, the rich *hacienda* (estate) owner became as autocratic as the feudal lords of Europe had been. He made his own laws and dominated everyone's life on his vast territory. Haciendas became like the company towns that steel, coal, and iron barons would rule over in mid-nineteenth-century America.

Answerable to nobody, the ranchers cut their expenses to the bone, reducing the wages of the vaqueros to as little as forty pesos a year. This was not nearly enough to sustain family life, so the vaqueros fell more and more deeply into debt. They had to buy food and other supplies on credit at the hacienda store, and then borrow for weddings, funerals, and the celebration of religious holidays. Many a vaquero passed through life without ever seeing cash, and his children inherited his debts. If this was a cowboy's life, who wanted it? Probably only those who had no other choice.

Cattle ranching in Mexico moved north into many parts of what is now known as the American Southwest—Arizona, New Mexico, and Texas—and on up into California. In the early 1800s the California ranches were much like the haciendas of old Mexico, the owners ruling their lands like feudal barons. The ranch owners lived a carefree life, little concerned with work, much concerned with pleasure. They treated their horses so indifferently that it shocked European travelers who visited the region. Edward Vischer, a German businessman who came to California in 1842, wrote home to his family:

The quickness and the agility of a Californian on horseback are a strange contrast to his usual languor. With utmost nonchalance he will saddle and harness his horse in the morning, chatting and smoking, using more time than is necessary. But after he has mounted his steed, often without using the stirrup, he is a different person. He never stops until he reaches his destination, no matter how far distant it may be. If the horse gets tired, the rider lassoes another at the next pasture, changes saddle, and continues his journey. Outside of notifying the owner of the borrowed horse, and releasing it to find its way back home, there are no formalities necessary. Traveling is nowhere easier and quicker than in California. A Californian will tear along the road as if it be a matter of life and death, yet he may only want to light a cigar at the house of a friend. He can talk for hours in front of a door, slumped in his saddle, until a sudden idea pulls him out of his indolence and causes a new outbreak of energy. Many spend days in this manner, going home only when they get hungry and are not invited to stay anywhere. If it happens that a man comes upon a gambling or drinking party, the ride is over for the day. Such a party often lasts twice twenty-four hours, until the last drop is consumed or the last coin gambled away. The poor animal remains saddled and tied to a post without fodder or water. When a ranchero comes to town to attend some festivity, the horse is treated in like manner. In spite of the long ride, it is left standing until the party is over, and then it has to carry its master home.

One reason for this brutal treatment of horses was their oversupply in California. The ranchers left their horses to care for themselves. Their contempt for the animals is captured in an old common saying that Vischer repeated: "Who told him to be a horse? Had he been born a bishop, he would have had no other work to do but give his blessing."

Richard Henry Dana, in his classic 1840 memoir, *Two Years Before the Mast,* described the Californians he met as "idle, thriftless people" who took as little care of the Indians as they did of their horses. They treated both like slaves.

The horse fared somewhat differently in Texas. Not long before Mexico won its independence from Spain in 1821, American colonists had begun to settle in Texas. Of the thousands who arrived, some farmers also raised cattle, but not on a large scale, and mostly to provide food for themselves. Only gradually did cattle ranching develop in Texas. Mexicans were hired as herdsmen; vaqueros caught and tamed mustangs or wild horses in order to sell or trade them to settlers.

Hunters tried to capture the small herds of wild horses that roamed the West. In this 1913 painting by Charles Russell, the riders have cornered the horses in a gully.

Mules, however, were often preferred by the early Texans. David Dary, in his book *Cowboy Culture*, tells why:

> Mules are more intelligent, surer-footed, and tougher than most horses. And their life span—thirty to thirty-five years—is ten to fifteen years longer than that of horses. Southerners found that mules can stand heat better than

horses, and they have the ability to do a third more work on a third less food on a hot day. A horse starts to get bothered when it gets hot, and then only gets hotter and more bothered. Although the Spanish had introduced mules in the New World, those ridden by the settlers were not of Spanish heritage. They were from the East, where George Washington began raising the first mules in the United States after Lafayette gave him a gift of a jack and two jennies. Both male and female mules, of course, are sterile and will not reproduce. A mule is out of a mare (female horse) and a jack (male ass). If a female ass (jenny) is mated with a male horse (stallion), the offspring is called a hinny, usually an inferior animal. It often takes an expert to distinguish a hinny from a mule; the only significant difference in appearance is that hinnies are slightly narrower at the heel. Being a hybrid animal, mules were not as plentiful as horses in early Texas, but they were more valuable.

Yet the horse, not the mule, soon became the favorite ranch animal. Most male ranch horses are gelded (castrated) before they are two years old. Reason? A gelding has an easier disposition than a stallion, which requires constant care and supervision. The common ranch horse runs on grass all its life and rarely needs the expensive services of a veterinarian. Gelded ranch horses are easier and cheaper to maintain than stallions. Properly trained, they become well adapted to the specialized skills called for on the ranch: calf roping and steer roping, bulldogging, cutting, and so on. The best ranch horses aren't limited to one specialty but can do any of these things.

For the cowboy, the quarter horse (so called because of its great speed over a quarter-mile distance) is by far the "doingest" breed. This chunky little speedster was first prized as a race horse in the colonial South. By the early 1800s the breed was moving westward, soon reaching the great cattle ranches of the frontier. It was a great treasure, that quarter horse. It could sprint with dazzling speed, it could turn on a dime, it could come to a sudden stop—just what the cowboy needed when working cattle.

Admired not only as a hardworking cow pony, it earned recognition as a great performer in racing, rodeos, and Western show events. A mix of European types with the wild herds and domesticated animals of America, this breed evolved into the short, sturdy-legged, muscular quarter horse we see now. It is America's most numerous and popular breed, and it ranks high internationally as well. People have used it for riding, jumping, hunting, racing, and polo.

When a cowboy is hired, either he may be asked to bring his own horse, or he will be furnished with a horse from the company stock. It is cheaper for the cowboy if he's given one, for a good horse can be quite costly. If he uses his own horse, he has his own basic tool; he knows what it can do, which can make his job easier. If he's riding the company's animal, it takes the cowboy some time to train it, and yet, just when all is going well, the rancher may snatch it away to sell it for a good price. As an old cowboy once told the author John R. Erickson, "Ride your own horses and improve your own stock. Then, when you leave this ranch, and move on to another, you'll have something to show for your time. 'Cause when you leave here, they ain't going to give you any more than a goodbye kiss."

Working on a ranch, the old-time cowboy usually needed more than one horse. The number depended on the size of the ranch, the kind of work to be done, and the nature of the land. If the land was mountainous, he would need more horses. The cowboy's group of horses—his string—might include two for morning, two for the afternoon, two for cutting (going into herds after cattle), and a night horse. Ranches that raised their own horses would let a cowboy use as many broncs as he wanted to handle. These were unbroken range horses, not useful in that condition for working cattle, but good enough to ride around the ranch. When broken, of course, they were worth more to the rancher.

Roundup time was twice a year. In the fall, it began around September 1 and lasted about two months. The time varied, of course, depending upon the size of the ranch and the conditions of work. Each man in the crew worked alone in a given area, herding the cattle back to the holding area. Then, around noon, the whole crew would meet near the chuck wagon, and while some held the herd, the others would eat and change horses. On their fresh mounts they'd spend the afternoon branding, earmarking, castrating, and doing anything else that needed to be done. This would go on day after day till all the ranch land had been worked over.

When the roundup was over, maybe one or two thousand head of the cattle would be herded to the railroad. That was usually a slow, tedious chore—if not interrupted by a stampede! At the railhead, it would take three or four days to load the cattle. That done, the cowboys were paid, and after they had a good time in town for a couple days, and shopped for clothes and whatever else they needed, the group would ride back to the ranch. Those hired just to work the roundup would pack their bedrolls, pick up their own horses, and take off.

By late fall the men who remained were settled into line camps scattered over the ranch land. Ahead lay a winter of mostly dull duties—repairing fences and corrals, digging postholes, inspecting water tanks, rescuing bogged-down cattle. Plenty to do, but little of it the romantic stuff fiction and the movies pretend is typical. In March all the crew would gather back at the ranch headquarters, to prepare for the spring roundup.

So these are the cowboys. What about cowgirls? Yes, there have always been women on the ranches, thousands of them. From the 1860s on, widows and other single women came west to stake out homesteads. They saw free land under the Homestead Act as their opportunity. Some went west married to cowboys and cattlemen, and ended up working more with the stock than with the washing. Working outside, on horseback and with cattle, provided an escape from domestic drudgery and broke the loneliness and isolation of the plains. With their experience on ranches, some women joined Wild West shows and rodeos. The women who could break broncs and win prizes became great celebrities. Calamity Jane was but one of many. She was a superb horsewoman and a crack shot. She drove cattle on the range and rode with the cavalry. The independence, self-confidence, and skills of these cowgirls made them favorites of the public.

Just as the capable women are usually left out of fiction and films about the old West, so too were the African Americans. Yet more than five thousand black cowboys worked on the plains during the three decades following the Civil War. They did as much on the ranches and trails as the cowboys who were white. But it was the whites who became folk heroes, not the blacks.

After the Civil War the black troopers of the 9th and 10th U.S. Cavalry also served in the West. They fought in the Indian wars and helped keep the peace among white cattle-men and settlers. They did much to make the expansion of the cattle empire possible. In their book-length study *The Negro Cowboy*, Philip Durham and Everett L. Jones wrote that the African-American cowboys "hunched in their saddles during the blizzards and thunderstorms, fought grass fires and turned stampedes, hunted wild mustangs and rode wild horses. Wolves threatened their cattle, and rattlesnakes crawled into their camps. Their lives were like those of all other cowboys—hard and dangerous."

The glory time of the cowboy was over by the end of the 1800s. Its tradition, however, still lingers in the fiction and films that touch the American imagination.

What about the cowhands of today? Except in a few scattered places, they are more likely farmers and mechanics than horse riders and ropers. When they have to ride, it's more often in a Jeep or pickup truck. If they need horses for certain work, they get to the job in a truck's cab, with the animals behind in horse trailers. As one historian puts it, "The old frontiers have vanished . . . and the old cowboy has disappeared from almost every range except the newsstand, the bandstand, the motion picture theater and the television screen."

Don't the cattle out on the range still need the attention of cowboys? Not really. The modern steer is raised by new methods that produce an expensively developed "machine" that makes tender beef from grass, grain, and special feeding mixtures. The modern steer is nothing like the feisty old longhorn, but is rather a docile beast, best handled slowly and gently by a man on foot. A steer pushed around by noisy cowhands on horseback would lose weight—which means the rancher would lose money. The old-time cowboy, says one Westerner, "would be as much at home on a slicked-up modern ranch as Daniel Boone at a debutante party."

EIGHT

Tractor and Truck Take Over

If it can be said that the horse in America had a Golden Age, it was a terribly short one. Only twenty years, from about 1890 to 1910. Although the industrial age had started long before this time, the old basic problem of transportation power had not yet been solved. Railroads laced the country together, and electric trolley cars moved through urban centers, but neither one could plow a field or haul building materials to a construction site. The modern truck and the tractor were still unknown.

What about the new automobiles? They could chug along city streets, but they could not make it over the mud holes and rocky ruts of country lanes. There were only 8,000 of them in 1900. They were expensive, and they constantly broke down.

Those horse-happy decades before 1910 are recalled by Prof. M. E. Ensminger:

During this era, everybody loved the horse. The town livery stable, watering trough, and hitching post were trademarks of each town and village. People wept when the horse fell on the icy street, and jailed men who beat or mistreated him. The oat-bag, carriage, wagon, buggy-whip, axle-grease, horseshoe, and horseshoe-nail industries were thriving and essential parts of the national economy. Every schoolboy knew and respected the village blacksmith.

Vast acreages of virgin soil in the Midwest and Far West were transformed after the Civil War into wheat, corn, and sugar-beet belts. Those belts ranged from five hundred to two thousand miles in width. Farmers needed massive horse-power to plant and harvest these crops. Oxen moved too slowly for the seasonal tasks on such huge farms; the horse was preferred for fieldwork and wagon tasks.

Then, in 1917, came a revolutionary change. Henry Ford, mass producer of cars at cheap prices, put the Fordson Tractor on the market. His tractors and trucks rolled off the assembly lines in stupendous numbers. Improved highways came soon after, built on a shared-cost basis by federal and

A giant harvester combine is pulled along the fields by a team of twenty-four horses in the Oregon of 1880.

local governments. Trucks soon took over from the horse the task of farm and city transportation, and by the time the Great Depression of the 1930s began, more than a million tractors were in use on American farms.

What did that change mean for horses? In 1919 there were 23 million of them; then year by year their number steadily diminished. When World War II began, in 1939, there were only 10 million horses in the United States, and by 1993, the number was 5,250,000.

Today there are only a few jobs left in which the horse can play a useful part. Surprisingly, even though city streets throughout much of the world are choked with motorized traffic, police horses are still in use and are thought to have some advantages. The police horse can inspire a certain amount of fear, often making it useful in controlling crowds and breaking up riots on crowded city streets. The mounted officer, riding on high, has a sweeping perspective on traffic problems, and his hand signals can be easily seen by motorists. In rural regions where streets and roads are rough going for cars, mounted police carry the law into mountain communities or across desert areas.

New York, where heavy traffic is a curse, has the largest mounted police force in the world. In 1993 command was assigned to Deputy Inspector Kathy E. Ryan, who was placed in charge of 146 officers. The city's police horses can work well into their twenties. When retired from duty, they live out their days on an upstate farm the cops call a horse heaven.

Police mounts come from many sources. Some are Thoroughbreds; others are saddle horses, or Morgans, or quarter horses. To obtain a uniform appearance, limits are

Deputy Inspector Kathy Ryan, head of New York City's mounted police force.

set for height, weight, color, and breed. When horses join the force, they are trained for the new job. They must especially learn to remain calm under difficult conditions. For weeks or months, they are barraged with sights and sounds to make them immune to disturbances.

When the horses have learned to remain calm despite gunshots, screaming sirens, blaring horns, and surging crowds, they are ready for assignment. In some forces only about a third of the horses make the grade. Once on the job there may be periods of little action. They rarely gallop, don't trot much, and stand still a lot.

Mounted officers have sometimes been used to control mass protest against social or economic conditions. Alarmed by large demonstrations, those in power have ordered mounted police or even cavalry to break them up. Men wielding clubs from atop rearing horses will terrify almost anybody.

The use of horses to enforce law and order is a very old practice. The innocent horses were often made to do the dirty work when people were tortured or executed. In some countries, when a person was convicted of a crime against the state and sentenced to death, four horses, one attached to each of the victim's arms and legs, were whipped into motion to tear the victim's body into four parts. This was called "drawing and quartering." Here in America, where lynchings were appallingly common well into the twentieth century, horses were made to assist in the crime. The victim was placed on a horse's back, and his neck was tied by a rope to the branch of a tree. The horse was whipped, making it plunge forward, leaving the rider to hang in the air, his neck broken.

One of the most notorious examples happened in 1819. A crowd of some sixty thousand men, women, and children was peacefully gathered on an open field in Manchester, England, to petition Parliament for reform laws. The authorities ordered a cavalry charge to break up the demonstration; eleven people were killed and four hundred injured. The Peterloo Massacre, as it was called, caused widespread anger at the government and added moral force to the movement for social reform.

NINE

Throroughbreds on the Racetrack

It's easy to imagine that horse racing might have been one of the earliest sports. Think of it—two early hunters on horseback, competitive as most of us are, out after deer, and suddenly one bets that his horse can outrun the other's. How more formal racing began, with fixed points for starts and stops, we don't know. One guess is that some Middle Eastern monarch thousands

A Persian king hunts the ibex, symbol of power. A gilded silver plate from the fifth century A.D.

A horse race in ancient Greece, painted on a vase around 500 B.C.

of years ago invented racing when he had both horses and time enough for such a sport.

Some scholars think chariot racing came first and that it had its origin in one of the early Olympic games. The games were celebrated as a national festival by the Greeks every four years, beginning nearly three thousand years ago. Only rich competitors took part in chariot races, because the cost of a chariot and the four horses needed to pull it was very high. Still, men like Alcibiades (c. 450–404 B.C.), an

Athenian statesman and general, entered no less than seven chariots in a race. Even kings eagerly competed for the prize—a garland of wild olive cut from a sacred tree. The first recorded race for mounted riders was also held during the Olympic games of 624 B.C. The prize was "a woman of well-rounded domestic skills"—a slave.

The Romans too offered chariot races in their circuses, but unlike the Greeks, Roman patricians would not themselves compete in public. Professionals held the reins, and winning drivers became as popular and rich as modern jockeys.

Great nerve and skill were needed to make the abrupt turns on the banked racecourses, and injuries were common, especially when as many as forty chariots careened down the track. A crowd of more than a hundred thousand spectators sat or stood around the arena, while slaves sold programs and some of them accepted bets for their masters. Often fierce arguments over the outcome of a race ended in bloody brawls.

As in the case of modern Thoroughbred racing, people committed crimes when big money was at stake. Horses were drugged or injured, drivers threatened or bribed, chariots sabotaged. At least two Roman emperors are known to have ordered the murder of charioteers scheduled to race against their own teams. Chariot racing got so dangerous that the star drivers paid bodyguards and food tasters to protect them against assault or food poisoning.

Hunting on horseback was a popular sport for both Greek and Roman aristocrats. The Greeks believed "it makes the body healthy and keeps men from growing old." The love for hunting and racing was carried to Britain by the Romans, and the sport thrived there throughout the long centuries of Roman occupation. Centuries later, Richard I entrenched it when he put up prize money in gold for the knights who won races. The passion for horse sports increased as the

The End of the Hunt, *a painting made in 1800.*

nobility set aside vast tracts of forestland for hunting parks, and both kings and queens followed the hounds from early childhood on. The monarchs established regular spring and autumn race meets, and some even competed themselves. No wonder racing became known as "the sport of kings."

Queen Victoria, the royal rider, at the beginning of her reign. An English lithograph, c. 1837.

History has known many talented horsewomen. Queen Elizabeth I of England (1533–1603) had that reputation, and is said to have kept riding until late in life. Diane de Poitiers (1499–1566) was an expert on horses and hunting. She got out of bed at three every morning to ride for hours. Queen Isabella of Spain (1451–1504) learned to ride at the age of three. She rode alongside her husband, King Ferdinand, in many a military campaign, wearing armor over her dress, and enduring extremes of heat and cold for hundreds of miles. The French Princess Anne, daughter of Louis XI (1423–1483), hunted wolves and wild boar. The six daughters of Charlemagne (768–814), riding astride, often accompanied their father on horseback tours of his kingdom. It was a long ride, from the Pyrenees into Italy.

Women rode in different styles, depending in part on their rank. The maidens of ancient Greece were said to ride naked to strengthen them so they could bear children easily. Much later, in Europe, lower-class women sat sideways or rode pillion— that is, on a pad or cushion on a whirlicote, a sort of wheeled litter, standing sideways.

In the early 1600s King Charles II sponsored a spring meet of racehorses in England, and soon after this, English settlers laid out a quarter-mile racetrack in Virginia. Between the purse and side bets, owners of winning horses might collect as much as $40,000 in gold, hogsheads of tobacco, bolts of cloth, and silver plate.

The South took quickly to the quarter-mile race. Southern horse breeders developed horses with strong legs, quick getaway, and spirit for the mad dash. Racing and breeding horses was an upper-class monopoly, "a sport only for gentlemen." But gradually it became more democratic. By 1800 racecourses could be found on the edges of most large towns and even many smaller ones.

The Civil War halted most of the racing in the devastated South. Thousands of horses were killed in the fighting, and some of the best breeding stock was wiped out. After the war, the rise of strict religious sects opposed to gambling and betting brought an end to racing in much of the region.

In the prosperous North, racing was still warmly supported. This was especially true of the horse-loving Irish, who were emigrating to America in great numbers due to the devastating potato famine in their homeland. It was the Irishman John Morrissey, once a prizefighter, who played a major role in founding at Saratoga Springs, New York, what today is the oldest and most aristocratic racecourse in the United States. Saratoga's famous medicinal hot springs had long made the town popular among the rich. Then, in 1864, with the opening of a beautiful Thoroughbred racetrack, it quickly became *the* resort for the fashionable crowd. A few years later Pimlico racetrack (now the site of the famous Preakness Stakes) was built near Baltimore, and then came Churchill Downs at Louisville, Kentucky, home of the Kentucky Derby.

African-American jockeys are a rarity now, but until the end of the nineteenth century most of the riders were black. Isaac Murphy, one of the best, won his first race in 1875, at the age of fourteen. He went on winning races, becoming the first jockey to ride winners three times in the Kentucky Derby, the most famous of all horse races. Because it had been the expected duty of slaves to care for the horses, there were black jockeys, handlers, trainers, and groomers everywhere from the early colonial days of the sport.

Even today, when everyone expects to travel on wheels or rails or wings, horses still rouse passions and make money flow in torrents. The richest men and women in the world compete to buy Thoroughbred horses. The three Maktoum

Galloping horses can reach speeds of thirty-five to forty-five miles an hour. When they are healthy, Thoroughbreds can keep up that speed for several miles. Why would a horse run so fast, when it isn't natural? The modern racehorse, kept much of the time penned up alone in its stall, is starved for powerful physical action. It is full of energy and ready to explode. When the starting gun of a race goes off, the horse rips off at high speed and keeps going at top pace until it is exhausted. If the horse gets tired before it reaches the finish line, it is passed by other horses. The typical Thoroughbred's energy is so exhausted in a race that the horse is usually unable to race again for days.

A curious fact is that speed records in horse racing are rarely broken; they've stayed much the same for the past century. Yet human athletes run faster and faster, breaking records more often. The reason, specialists say, is that the modern race horse was perfected over the past two hundred years until a certain limit in speed was reached. Unless the gene pool is widened experimentally, the situation isn't likely to change.

An 1878 poster announces trotting races in Illinois.

brothers, from the royal family of Dubai, a small but oil-rich country in the Middle East, spend huge sums buying and training racehorses. They have paid nearly one million dollars for a yearling. At one sale they spent $47 million for animals to add to their breeding stock of a thousand horses.

When horses become so valuable, corruption sets in. Not long ago a criminal was caught who admitted that over a ten-year period he had killed fifteen horses after slipping into American stables and barns during the middle of the night. The rich owners of the horses paid him $5,000 for

Jockey Julie Krone pats her horse as they win the Belmont Stakes. Krone was the first woman to win a Triple Crown race.

each murder, and then pocketed between ten thousand and several hundred thousand dollars per horse in insurance money. The hired killer did his work in such a way that the insurance companies were convinced that the horses died of illnesses or accidents.

On the legitimate side, the price of buying, breeding, and training horses has shot up so high that several stock companies have been formed just for investment in horses. Now business speculators play the horses on Wall Street.

TEN

In Folklore,
Art, and Myth

We've seen how well the horse has served its master for thousands of years, in times of peace as well as war. No wonder, then, that in folklore, art, and myth the horse has a special place of honor. It is a sign of the great affection people have always felt for the horse that it rarely has a bad or evil image.

In ancient times the horse was associated with emblems of creative life, such as the sun being drawn in its chariot by celestial horses on its daily passage across the skies. Both the ancient Norse people and the Romans had a similar myth— of the moon being towed through the dark heavens.

In old Irish belief, riding a white horse gave the rider a special gift of knowing how to treat physical ailments, but to the Saxon King Alfred, a white horse symbolized victory.

The legendary Trojan horse moves into the besieged city of Troy, as imagined by Giovanni Tiepolo, a Venetian painter of the eighteenth century.

When he conquered the Danes in the ninth century, he had a huge white horse, 374 feet long and 120 feet high, carved on a steep chalk cliff on the Berkshire Down in England.

The Trojan Horse is folklore recorded in Homer's great poem the *Iliad.* The war between the Greeks and the people of Troy (c. 1240 B.C.) is the setting for the poem. The Greeks besieged Troy for ten years, but the city was so strongly fortified that it did not fall. In desperation the Greeks turned from arms to deceit. They pretended to abandon their camp at the foot of Troy's walls, but left a huge wooden horse behind. The Trojans came out and dragged the horse into their city. Greek warriors, hidden inside the wooden horse, sneaked out and opened the city's gates to the Greek army. It was the end of Troy and the beginning of a metaphor.

The Old Testament tells the story of how the early Israelites were favored by the intervention of divine horses. Second Kings vii tells that when the Israelites were about to be wiped out by a huge force of Syrians, the Lord made the army of the Syrians imagine that they heard the noise of a great mass of enemy horsemen coming on; it caused the frightened Syrians to flee.

Much later, in the eighteenth century, the Irish writer Jonathan Swift described in his satirical masterpiece *Gulliver's Travels* a race of horses gifted with reason, speech, and noble qualities. Called the Houyhnhnms, they ruled over the brutish humans, called Yahoos.

In the literature of many lands, horse and rider are deeply interwoven. Many a reader has thrilled to Washington Irving's *The Legend of Sleepy Hollow*, with its headless horseman galloping through the wild forests along the banks of the Hudson River.

Lord Byron's poem *Mazeppa* is the tale of a Polish noble-man whose life is saved by a wild horse. In Anna Sewell's

The cover of Washington Irving's Legend of Sleepy Hollow *illustrated by Arthur Rackham.*

celebrated tale *Black Beauty*, the narrator is a horse—a device that projects human emotions and thinking upon an animal.

There is no end to horse tales: *My Friend Flicka, National Velvet, The Red Pony*, to name but a few, and the steady stream of Westerns by such immensely popular writers as Zane Grey and Will James. Cowboy sagas are more often encountered

Black Bess was one of England's most famous horses. She was ridden not by a great jockey but by a notorious highwayman, Dick Turpin. A farmer's son, he took to stealing sheep, turned to smuggling, then found his true niche as a highwayman. In Turpin's day—the early eighteenth century—highwaymen were "as common as crows." Riding Black Bess, Turpin robbed travelers on the various roads leading out of London. When Black Bess tired on their dashing raids, he would refresh her with strong ale. Caught at last, and tried, Turpin died in style. He bought himself a new suit and new shoes just before his execution, hired five men to follow him to the grave as mourners, and in the cart on the way to his hanging bowed graciously to the spectators lining the road. He chatted calmly with the hangman while standing on the platform, then jumped gracefully into oblivion. "It was necessary to the success and even to the safety of the highwayman that he should be a bold and skillful rider," wrote Lord Macaulay, "and that his manners and appearance should be such as suited the master of a fine horse. He therefore held an aristocratical position in the community of thieves, appeared at fashionable coffeeehouses and gaming houses, and betted with men of quality on the race ground." A criminal elite, the highwaymen were glorified in legends, ballads, novels, and plays.

The rocking horse amused Greek and Roman children of antiquity, but the name we know it by comes from a breed of Irish horses enjoyed for their comfortable gait. These gentle horses, called hobbies, were popular in England at least six hundred years ago. Children claimed the name of hobbyhorse for their toy.

Prince August Wilhelm of Germany, in a photograph of 1890.

nowadays on TV or in the movies than on the printed page. Parents and grandparents probably recall the famous horses ridden by the cowboy stars of the movies they grew up on—Tom Mix and his Tony, or Roy Rogers and his Trigger.

Graphic artists have always found horses a superb subject for painting and sculpture. On the ceiling of the famous cave discovered in 1879 at Altamira, Spain, there are beautifully sketched figures of horses made by Stone Age people in the earliest period of human culture. The art of the ancient cultures of North Africa, Persia, India, and China depicts horses, and sculptors in classical Greece carved magnificent horses for the frieze on the Parthenon in Athens some 2,500 years ago. Later, horses figured vividly in medieval illuminated manuscripts.

Many artists of the Renaissance, such as Leonardo da Vinci, Paolo Ucello, Michelangelo Caravaggio, and Albrecht Dürer, chose the horse as a subject. In more recent centuries artists like Rembrandt van Rijn, Francisco Goya, Edgar Degas, Edouard Manet, Henri Toulouse-Lautrec, Marc Chagall, and Pablo Picasso used brush or chisel to capture the power and beauty of the animal.

In Greek mythology centaurs play lively roles. Depicted as half man, half horse, centaurs symbolized the destructive

The Large Horse, *an example of great animals ridden by knights in the medieval era, engraved by the German artist Albrecht Dürer.*

The Polish Rider, *a painting by the Dutch master Rembrandt van Rijn.*

and uncontrollable forces of nature. Sometimes centaurs were shown as being among the guardians of Hell. Around 1000 B.C. artists drew the centaur as a creature with the body and legs of a horse, but with a man's torso, arms, and head, the face bearded. Myth held that the centaurs taught riding and battle skills to Hercules and Achilles, and that they told Jason what route to take on his quest for the Golden Fleece. No doubt the Greek legend of a creature that was half man, half horse preserves a timeless memory—the reaction of the early Greeks when they first saw barbarians from the north invading their lands on the backs of horses.

Horselike creatures appeared in myths in medieval times too. The unicorn was as familiar a creature to the people of the Middle Ages as the centaur was to the Greeks. The unicorn was a mythical beast that looked like a young horse with a pointed, spiraling horn jutting from the middle of its forehead. Sometimes there were even more fanciful images of unicorns, showing them with the head, neck, and body of a horse, the legs of a stag, and the tail of a lion, but always with a long, twisted horn projecting from the forehead.

Unicorns were said to have magical powers. Drinking from a cup made of a unicorn's horn would protect you from poisoning—a common means of doing away with enemies in those days. The literature of this era is rich in stories of unicorns doing fantastic deeds. In one story a unicorn named Bayard carries four men on his back to help them race away from an emperor's wrath.

Many artists drew their vision of the horse from legends.

For the ancient Greeks, who based their epic literature upon myth, the horse almost always figured as a symbol of the gods' generosity toward humans. Myth held that the first horse emerged from the sea, created by the god Poseidon, who reigned over the oceans. What lay behind that belief? Perhaps it was born some four thousand years ago, when an enemy force attacked the Mediterranean island of Crete. The assault ships may have carried horses as well as warriors, and when the boats neared the beach, the cavalrymen probably rode their horses ashore. One can believe that the awesome first sight of a horse racing through the surf in a wild flurry of foam gave birth to the myth of the winged wonder horse called Pegasus.

The divine winged horse was caught by Athena, daughter of the great god Zeus. She herself became the goddess of both war and wisdom. Pegasus was a terrible wild creature, untamed and untamable by mortals. Only Athena could control him. She placed Pegasus in the care of the Muses— the nine goddesses of the arts.

Now the myth brings in a mortal warrior, Bellerophon. Known to be a great hero, he had been set what seemed an impossible task. Ravaging the countryside was a fire-breathing monster called the Chimera. It had the head of a

Statue of a unicorn with a dog on its back, made in Germany about A.D. 1400.

lion, the body of a goat, and the tail of a serpent. King
Iobates demanded that Bellerophon live up to his reputation
and slay the monster. But how would he catch it? One night

Athena appeared to him in a vision and said that she would help. She gave Bellerophon a golden bridle, and with that treasure the hero was able to mount Pegasus. Galloping on the back of the winged horse, he caught up with the monster and killed it. In reward, Iobates gave Bellerophon his daughter in marriage, and half his kingly power.

But Bellerophon's last years were unhappy. The gods came to hate him (out of envy?), his son and daughter died young, and the hero sank into deep depression. Finding no pleasure in the company of mere mortals, he saddled the winged Pegasus once more and set out on a flight to heaven to visit the gods on Mount Olympus. Zeus was so angered by the arrogance of Bellerophon that he sent a gadfly to sting Pegasus under the tail. The winged horse reeled in the sky, hurling Bellerophon back to earth. The fall left him lame and blind, fated to wander friendless and alone. Pegasus remained in the stable of Zeus, summoned now and then by the god to carry thunderbolts through the sky.

Pegasus also appears in Greek mythology as Poseidon's instrument for revealing the source of fresh water to humankind. When the winged horse stamped on the earth, his hoofbeats caused the waters of a sacred spring to gush forth. The story may have its roots in the fact that the Siberian wild horse, the Przewalski, paws the earth in summertime at points it instinctively, or from experience, knows to be waterholes.

In some cultures the horse is given the special honor of carrying heroic or divine persons to paradise. In Norse mythology heroes killed in combat rode up to Valhalla on the horses of the Valkyries, warrior maidens entrusted with their souls. In Muslim tradition, Mohammed is said to have ascended to heaven on a winged horse named Al Borak.

Wherever the horse appears in mythology, it is usually associated with power or wisdom, and these qualities are often transferred to humans who can master the creature. In Homer's *Iliad,* one of the earliest known works of literature, the heroic son of King Priam of Troy is paid lyrical tribute as "horse-taming Hector."

Even in more recent times, some people have been said to be blessed by the intervention of divine horses and riders. In the Battle of Lake Regillus in 496 B.C., Castor and Pollux, the twin sons of Zeus, themselves equestrian gods, came to the aid of the beleaguered Romans and helped them overcome the enemy. About two thousand years later, Saint James, the patron saint of horsemen, appeared on horseback several times to help the Spanish drive out the Moors. In the same era, the Archangel Michael appeared on horseback to Joan of Arc, inspiring her to lead the French to victory over the English.

Sometimes a wonder horse became the symbol of hope for an oppressed people. Sharatz, a horse famed for his power—he could leap four lance-lengths forward and three upward—was the favorite mount of King Marko of the Serbs in the fourteenth century. The two led the Serbian forces in resistance to the domination of the Turks. Sharatz, the story goes, would trample Turkish cavalrymen into the earth and bite off the ears of their horses. The legend says that King Marko never died, but sleeps in a mountain cavern, with Sharatz at his side, waiting for the call to fight again for freedom.

It may well be true, as many historians claim, that myth is history dimly remembered. The deeds of the horse in mythology, then—almost always heroic and good—only reflect what the horse truly has contributed to civilization.

Bibliography
A Note on Sources
Index

The principal sources for this book are listed alphabetically. Then, chapter by chapter, those sources relied on for the contents of that chapter are singled out, using the last name of the author. Such a list is inevitably uneven. Information may be found scattered through the files of periodicals or in corners of books mainly focused on other subjects.

Bibliography

Andrewes, Antony. *The Greeks.* New York: Norton, 1978.

Bloch, Marc. *Life and Work in Medieval Europe.* New York: Harper, 1969.

Braider, Donald. *The Life, History and Magic of the Horse.* New York: Grosset, 1973.

Bransted, Johannes. *The Vikings.* Baltimore: Penguin, 1960.

Braudel, Fernand. *Capitalism and Material Life, 1400–1800.* New York: Harper, 1975.

———. *The Mediterranean and the Medieval World in the Age of Phillip II.* New York: Harper, 1973.

———. *The Wheels of Commerce.* New York: Harper, 1982.

Burckhardt, Jacob. *The Civilization of the Rennaissance in Italy.* New York: Phaidon, 1965.

Campbell, Judith. *Horses and Ponies.* New York: Bantam, 1972.

Cavalli-Sforza, Luigi Luca. "A Geneticist Maps Ancient Migrations." *The New York Times,* July 27, 1993.

Coleman, Jane C. "A Horsewoman Looks at Historical Fiction." *Authors Guild Bulletin*, Spring 1993.

Crowell, Pers. *Cavalcade of American Horses*. New York: McGraw, 1951.

Curwen, E. Cecil. *Plough and Pasture*. London: Cobbett, 1946.

Dary, David. *Cowboy Culture*. New York: Knopf, 1981.

Davidson, Marshall. *Life in America*. Boston: Houghton, 1951.

Disston, Harry. *Know About Horses*. New York: Bramhall, 1961.

Driver, Harold E. *Indians in North America*. Chicago: University of Chicago, 1969.

Durham, Philip, and Everett L. Jones. *The Negro Cowboys*. Lincoln, Neb.: University of Nebraska, 1965.

Ensminger, M. E. *Horses and Horsemanship*. Danville, Ill.: Interstate, 1969.

Erickson, John R. *The Modern Cowboy*. Lincoln, Neb.: University of Nebraska, 1981.

Farb, Peter. *Man's Rise to Civilization, As Shown by the Indians of North America*. New York: Dutton, 1968.

Gernet, Jacques. *A History of Chinese Civilization*. New York: Cambridge University, 1982.

Hibben, Frank C. *The Lost Americans*. New York: Crowell, 1946.

Howard, Robert West. *The Horse in America*. Chicago: Follett, 1965.

Jarrett, Derek. *England in the Age of Hogarth*. New Haven: Yale University, 1986.

Jordan, Teresa. *Cowgirls: Women of the American West*. New York: Anchor, 1982.

Josephy, Alvin M., Jr., ed. *American Heritage Book of Indians*. New York: American Heritage, 1961.

Keegan, John. *A History of Warfare.* New York: Knopf, 1993.

Larkin, Jack. *The Reshaping of Everyday Life, 1790–1840.* New York: Harper, 1988.

Lear, Martha Weinman. "She's No Jockette." *The New York Times,* July 25, 1993.

Lowie, Robert H. *Indians of the Plains.* New York: McGraw 1954.

Morris, Pamela M., and Nerea Kugli. *Horses of the World.* New York: Bounty, 1973.

Nabokov, Peter, ed. *Native American Testimony.* New York: Crowell, 1978.

The New Yorker, Talk of the Town. "The Early Horse." August 18, 1980.

Nye, Nelson C. *Your Western Horse.* New York: Barnes, 1963.

Osborne, Walter D., and Patricia H. Johnson. *The Treasury of Horses.* New York: Ridge, 1966.

Parry, J. H. *The Age of the Renaissance.* New York: Mentor, 1963.

Possehl, Suzanne. "Rare Przewalski's Horse Returns to the Harsh Mongolian Steppe." *The New York Times,* October 4, 1994.

Reynolds, Robert L. *Europe Emerges: 1600–1750.* Madison, Wisc.: University of Wisconsin, 1957.

Weber, Philip, and Stanley M. Jepson. *Heroes in Harness: The Heavy Horse.* New York: Barnes, 1979.

Wilford, John Noble. "Remaking the Wheel: Evolution of the Chariot." *The New York Times,* February 22, 1994.

Wolf, Eric R. *Europe and the People Without History.* Berkeley, Calif.: University of Calfornia, 1982.

A Note on Sources

CHAPTER ONE

Descriptions of the nature of the horse and of its evolution may be found in a great many sources. I used chiefly Morris, Ensminger, Crowell, Reynolds, Possehl, and Osborne.

CHAPTER TWO

The findings at the dig in Dereivka were described in the *New Yorker* interview with the archaeozoologist. For how chariots were developed and their role in migration and warfare, see Gernet, Wilford, Braider, Ensminger, Morris, Crowell, Andrewes, Reynolds, Howard, and Keegan.

CHAPTER THREE

On nomads, Gernet; on Islam, Braudel's *Mediterrean;* on medieval jousting, Osborne; on cavalry, Keegan, Morris, and Braudel's *Capitalism.*

CHAPTER FOUR

The literature of the American Civil War is immense. The role of cavalry on both sides is covered in comprehensive histories of that war, in specialized accounts of that branch of the military, and in biographies of great cavalry commanders. My discussion came from my earlier work done on the Civil War.

CHAPTER FIVE

The gradual replacement of human muscle by horse power is covered in rich detail in many studies. I used chiefly Braudel's *Capitalism*, his *Wheels*, and his *Mediterranean*, but also Parry, Osborne, Howard, Ensminger, Weber, Larkin, and Braider.

CHAPTER SIX

For the story of how horses returned to the New World in the ships of the conquistadors, I used Howard, Braider, and Parry. The revolutionary role of the horse in Indian life is a vital part of almost any study of the Indians. Those relied on here are Farb, Driver, Hibben, Josephy, Lowie, and Nabokov.

CHAPTER SEVEN

The details on the cowboy's use of the horse come from Dary, Durham, Erickson, Jordan, and Nye.

CHAPTER EIGHT

The fading out of the horse as a utilitarian animal is covered in Ensminger, Howard, Osborne, and Weber. The police horse is described in Braider, Disston, and Osborne, and in recent reports in *The New York Times*.

CHAPTER NINE

The pleasure the horse has provided in recreation and amusement is covered in a great many books about individual sports. Braider and Osborne are quite comprehensive, and Morris, Ensminger, Osborne, Campbell, and Howard add details. *The New York Times* almost daily covers horse sports, especially racing. Durham discusses black jockeys, and Davidson describes racing in early America.

CHAPTER TEN

Almost any book about folklore, myth, legend, and literature will inevitably have horses riding through it. My material comes from too many scattered sources for full listing. But most useful for summaries were Braider, Osborne, and Howard.

Index

Page references to illustrations are in *italics*.

About the Author

Milton Meltzer completed *The Amazing Potato* and *Gold* and then turned to the horse as the final part of his trilogy on the three kingdoms of nature—vegetable, mineral, and animal—and how they have shaped human history. He has published nearly ninety books for young people and adults in the fields of history, biography, and social reform. He has written and edited for newspapers, magazines, radio, television, and films.

Among the many honors for his books are five nominations for the National Book Award. He has won the Christopher, Jane Addams, Carter G. Woodson, Jefferson Cup, Washington Book Guild, Olive Branch, and Golden Kite awards. Many of his books have been chosen for the honor lists of the American Library Association, the National Council of Teachers of English, the National Council for the Social Studies, and the New York Public Library's annual Books for the Teen Age.

Born in Worcester, Massachusetts, Mr. Meltzer was educated at Columbia University. He lives with his wife in New York City. They have two daughters and two grandsons.